Million Dollar Service Startup

Step by Step Systems to Grow your Service Company to $1,000,000

By John Michael McDonald Jr

John McDonald Jr Publishing

Copyright © 2025 John Michael McDonald Jr.
All rights reserved.

No part of this book may be reproduced, stored in a retrieval system, or transmitted in any form or by any means—electronic, mechanical, photocopying, recording, or otherwise—without the prior written permission of the publisher, except in the case of brief quotations used in reviews or articles.

This book is intended for educational and informational purposes only. It does not constitute legal, financial, tax, or professional advice. Readers should consult qualified professionals before making business, financial, or legal decisions. The author and publisher disclaim any liability arising directly or indirectly from the use of this book.

Million Dollar Service Startup
First edition

ISBN: 979-8-9939660-0-7

John McDonald Jr Publishing
Fountain Inn, South Carolina

Printed in the United States of America

Dedication

To my daughter, whose strength inspires me every day. May you continue to walk in courage, resilience, and wisdom. You help me see that my purpose is to serve others, and I am forever grateful to God for the gift of borrowing you. The world is yours. I love you unconditionally.

To my parents, who instilled in me a hard work ethic and the belief that I can do anything, and who taught me to attack life without limits. That belief has been essential in every part of my journey. Thank you, Mom and Dad

Acknowledgements

Thank you to every employee, past and present, who has been part of Fabtech Solutions team. You have trusted me with the direction of your careers and families—and I do not take that responsibility lightly. I am also deeply grateful to the friends and mentors who continue to support me and sharpen me into a better version of myself. In a journey that can feel lonely sometimes, your advice, wisdom, honest criticism, and accountability have helped light the path forward more than you know.

Introduction

This book exists for one reason: to help you grow your service business from zero to $1 million in revenue faster than I did. You'll find countless business books on the market, and probably like you, I've spent years soaking in their lessons—reading, hiring coaches and mentors, listening to every podcast and watching every business video I could find on YouTube. But real growth comes from action, and what you hold here is the product of a long journey of putting those lessons into practice—ultimately reaching the milestone of $1 million in annual service revenue.

Along the way, one principle became non-negotiable for me: you don't improve what you don't measure. In this book, you'll see that theme repeated—tracking numbers, watching trends, and using data to drive better decisions inside your service business.

I have designed this book to be direct, packed into 11 short chapters with action items. Take what you need, apply it quickly, and then get back to building your business. I look forward to hearing about your wins.

Transparency matters. My main company Fabtech Solutions has three revenue streams: sales, service, and parts. We crossed the 1 million mark in total revenue at year three, but the path to $1 million in service-specific revenue was full of detours. I was pulled in many directions—juggling multiple parts of the business at once—which slowed my progress. My advice to you:

avoid these distractions if you can. Focus intently on growing your service revenue first. Once you hit your goals and have strong department managers, you can expand into new streams and integrate vertically. Too many revenue streams early on will dilute your growth.

The roadmap ahead comes from real-world lessons—not theory. Read or listen fast, take action, and let's build your $1 million service business together.

Table of Contents

Introduction — 5
Chapter 1: Becoming Unemployable — 12
- Narrative: Why Start a Company? — 13
- Lessons Learned: Paths Forward and Leadership Evolution — 13
- Actionable Advice: Building Paths and Structure — 14
- Practical Steps: Becoming a True Leader — 15
- What to Measure in This Stage — 16
- Reflection Questions for Readers — 16
- Closing Thoughts — 17

Chapter 2: Marketing 101 — 18
- Learning From Mistakes — 18
- Make a Plan — 19
- A Simple Example — 19
- Social Media Is My Favorite Form of Marketing — 20
- Simple Steps for Better Marketing — 21
- What to Measure in Marketing — 22
- Reflection Questions — 22
- What Matters Most — 22

Chapter 3: When to Hire — 24
- The Struggle of Doing It All — 24

Why Hiring Matters	24
How to Know When the Time Is Right	25
Planning Your First (or Next) Hire	25
Finding the Right Person	26
Training New Team Members	27
Growing as a Leader	27
Practical Steps for Hiring	28
What to Measure Around Hiring	28
Reflection Questions	29
Closing Thoughts	29
Chapter 4: When to Fire	**30**
Why Terminate Someone	30
Signs It Is Time to Let Someone Go	30
Firing Is Not About Anger	31
The Right Way to Fire Someone	31
Learning From Every Firing	32
Helping Your Team Move Forward	33
Practical Tips	33
What to Measure Around Firing	34
Reflection Questions	34
Closing Thoughts	35
Chapter 5: Attracting Talent	**36**

Why Talent Matters	36
Common Mistakes When Attracting Talent	36
How to Attract the Right Talent	37
1. Show Off Your Company's Strengths	37
2. Use Word of Mouth and Social Media	37
3. Make a Clear Job Posting	38
4. Treat Each Candidate Well	38
5. Offer Training and Growth	39
6. Reward Good Work	39
When You Can't Find Talent	39
What to Measure Around Attracting Talent	40
Reflection Questions	40
Final Thoughts	41
Chapter 6: Employee Handbook	**41**
Why Rules and Policies Matter	42
Common Mistakes with Handbooks	42
How to Build Your Employee Handbook	43
Getting Feedback and Keeping It Alive	44
Communicating Expectations	44
Being Consistent and Fair	45
What to Measure Around Policies	45
Reflection Questions	46

Final Thoughts	46

Chapter 7: Pay — Performance-Driven Compensation
48

What Is Performance Pay?	48
Why Use Performance Pay?	49
Common Mistakes to Avoid	49
Setting Up a Simple, Fair System	50
Tracking Results and Giving Feedback	51
Supporting Employees Who Miss Goals	51
Celebrating and Recognizing Success	52
What to Measure in Performance Pay	52
Reflection Questions	53
Final Thoughts	53

Chapter 8: Systems and Numbers 54

Why Systems Matter	54
Common Mistakes	54
Start With Your Critical Paths	55
Make Systems Real for Your Team	56
Numbers: What to Measure	56
Turning Data into Decisions	57
Practical Steps	57
Reflection Questions	58
Final Thoughts	58

Chapter 9: Protecting Profit and Pricing your Service 58

Why Profit Comes First 59
Common Money Traps 59
Know Your Numbers 60
Price Like a Real Business 60
Control Overhead and Creep 61
Tighten Cash Flow 62
What to Measure Around Profit and Cash 62
Practical Steps 63
Reflection Questions 63
Final Thoughts 63

Chapter 10: Ticket Takers vs. Drivers 64

Ticket Takers: Just Doing the Job 64
Drivers: Moving the Business Forward 64
How to Spot the Difference 65
Turning Ticket Takers into Drivers 65
When a Ticket Taker Should Stay a Ticket Taker 66
When It's Time to Move On 66
What to Measure Around People 67
Practical Steps 67
Reflection Questions 68
Final Thoughts 68

Chapter 11: Bringing It All Together   69

   Your Million-Dollar Service Engine   69

   Build a 12-Month Roadmap   70

   Establish a Weekly Rhythm   71

   Your Core Scoreboard   72

   Expect Resistance and Keep Going   73

   Reflection and Next Steps   74

   Final Words   74

Chapter 1: Becoming Unemployable

Narrative: Why Start a Company?

If you picked up this book, chances are you are a technician, tradesman, or service pro who is tired of being told what to do by people who have never done the work. You want more control, more upside, and a business that can take care of your family instead of just covering the bills.

That was me. I did not start Fabtech Solutions because I dreamed of becoming a CEO. I started because I wanted autonomy. I was tired of micromanagers, politics, and ceilings on my income. Owning a service business looked like freedom—until I realized I had simply traded one boss for many. I now worked for employees, customers, vendors, and the bank.

The bigger lesson: starting a company is not just about escaping a job you hate. It is about becoming the kind of leader people actually want to follow. That shift—from "I want freedom" to "I am responsible for others' futures"—is what this chapter is really about.

Lessons Learned: Paths Forward and Leadership Evolution

In the early days, my entire focus was survival. Get work. Do the work. Get paid. Repeat. I did not think about leadership development, culture, or long-term career paths for employees. My first hire quit because he could not see a future at Fabtech—and he was right. I had no clear path for him beyond "help me get through this week."

That forced me to confront a hard truth: if people cannot see where they are going in your company, they will leave. Ironically, I had left my previous job for the exact same reason. Employees want to know three things:

- Where am I today?
- Where could I be in a year or two?
- What has to happen for me to get there?

As Fabtech grew, I realized that becoming "unemployable" is not about having no boss. It is about becoming the person who sets a vision, lives it out, and earns enough respect that good people choose to stay. That required me to level up mentally, physically, spiritually, and financially. People will not follow someone who is undisciplined, broke, and bitter. They follow someone who is growing.

Actionable Advice: Building Paths and Structure

To build a million-dollar service startup, you must stop thinking like a solo operator and start thinking like a builder of people and systems. That starts with paths—clear advancement routes inside your company.

Create simple, written paths for each role: helper, technician, senior tech, lead, manager. For every step, define:

- Skills required
- Behaviors expected
- Pay range or compensation structure

Review these paths with your team regularly. When people know the target and the rules of the game, they can aim their effort in the right direction instead of guessing.

Practical Steps: Becoming a True Leader

Here are practical, measurable ways to start leading instead of just grinding:

- **Define roles and paths.** Write out each position and what "next level" looks like in skills, responsibility, and pay.
- **Schedule one-on-ones.** Meet with each team member at least quarterly to discuss goals, performance, and what they want long term. Take notes and follow up.
- **Invest in yourself.** Read one leadership or business book per month, hire a coach if you can, and treat your health like part of your job. A tired, unhealthy owner makes poor decisions.
- **Create simple scorecards.** For yourself and for key roles, track a handful of numbers every week: revenue produced, jobs completed, callbacks, reviews, on-time performance. You do not improve what you do not measure.
- **Model the standard.** Show up early. Own your mistakes. Admit when you do not know something. People copy what you do, not what you post on the wall.

What to Measure in This Stage

To live out the "measure to improve" principle from the introduction, start tracking:

- **Your personal development time:** hours per week spent learning (books, courses, coaching).
- **Employee retention:** how many people stay 12+ months.
- **Advancement:** how many team members move up at least one level per year.
- **Leadership touchpoints:** number of one-on-ones or coaching conversations you have each month.

You do not need fancy software. A simple spreadsheet or notebook is enough. What matters is that you see trends and adjust.

Reflection Questions for Readers

- Why did you start (or want to start) your service company, and what core value is driving you today?
- Can your current or future employees clearly see a path forward in your business?
- Are you growing fast enough as a leader to justify others following you? Where are you coasting?
- What are the top three metrics you will start measuring this week to improve your leadership and team development?
- Looking one year ahead, what do you want your team to say about working for you?

Closing Thoughts

Becoming unemployable is not about never having a boss again. It is about becoming a builder of people, a steward of opportunity, and a leader worth following. The sacrifice is real—less comfort now for a better company (and life) later. But if you commit to growth, define clear paths, and measure what matters, you can build a million-dollar service startup that people are proud to be part of.

Chapter 2: Marketing 101

Marketing is how people who need you actually find you. When most service owners say, "We grow by word of mouth," what they really mean is, "We don't have a real marketing plan, and we're hoping the phone keeps ringing." Hope is not a strategy. If you want a million-dollar service startup, you need simple, consistent, measurable marketing.

Learning From Mistakes

When I started Fabtech Solutions, I equated "good marketing" with big, loud ideas. I wanted attention. Sometimes that worked, but a lot of the time it didn't. I would spend time and money on a flyer, email, or ad, feel good about how it looked, and then never check whether it actually produced revenue.

Eventually, I realized my real problem: I wasn't treating marketing like a system. I wasn't tracking results, I wasn't asking for feedback, and I wasn't learning from what the numbers were telling me. Once I slowed down, involved my team in reviewing messages before they went out, and started measuring outcomes, things changed.

Instead of asking, "Did people like this?" we started asking, "What did this do?" If a campaign brought in calls, quotes, and booked work, we kept it and refined it. If it didn't move any numbers, we fixed it or killed it. Emotion stopped leading; data did.

Make a Plan

Good marketing is just a clear plan you repeat. Before launching anything—post, mailer, email, ad—answer four simple questions:

1. What are we promoting?
   One service, one offer, one call to action.
2. Where are we sharing it?
   Email list, Facebook, Instagram, door hangers, job-site signs, etc.
3. How long are we running it?
   Weekend promo, 14-day push, or 30-day campaign.
4. How will we know it worked?
   Calls, form fills, quotes, jobs, and revenue.

Write this on a one-page "campaign sheet." Use the same logo, colors, and phrases across everything so customers recognize you instantly in their feed, inbox, or mailbox. Your goal isn't to be clever—it's to be consistent and easy to remember.

A Simple Example

Let's say you want to fill your slow season with maintenance work:

- Offer: "$99 pre-season tune-up—limited spots this month."
- Channels: 2 emails, 8 social posts, a banner on trucks, and a script for whoever is answering the phone.
- Time frame: 30 days.

- Metrics: number of calls, tune-ups booked, and revenue from those customers.

At the end of the month, you review the numbers. If the campaign generated profitable work and some long-term customers, you schedule it again next year. If not, you change the offer, the channel, or the timing—and test again. That is how real marketing systems are built.

Social Media Is My Favorite Form of Marketing

Social media is still the most powerful **free** tool you have. Before owning a business, I had no social media presence. Now it's one of my main levers for awareness and trust. Platforms like Facebook, Instagram, TikTok, LinkedIn, and YouTube let you:

- Show real work in progress.
- Highlight your team and customers.
- Educate people on the problems you solve.
- Stay in front of your market every day at no cost beyond your time.

You do not need fancy production or viral dances. You need to be visible and honest. Post:

- Before/after photos.
- Short tips ("One thing to check before you call a tech").
- Customer testimonials.
- Behind-the-scenes shots of training, team meetings, or job-site setups.

If social media isn't your thing, assign it to a trusted employee or hire an agency—but commit at least six months, because agencies need time to learn your brand and audience.

Simple Steps for Better Marketing

1. Claim your real estate.
   Make sure your business name, logo, phone, and website are consistent on Google, Facebook, Instagram, and any major platform your customers use.
2. Post with a rhythm.
   Start with 3–5 posts per week. Mix jobs, team, tips, offers, and testimonials so people see the full picture of your business.
3. Use clear calls to action.
   End posts and emails with a simple direction: "Call to schedule," "Click to request a quote," or "Message us to book."
4. Track basic numbers.
   - **Website:** visitors and form fills.
   - **Social:** reach, link clicks, DMs that become jobs.
   - **Phone:** calls tied to specific campaigns (ask, "How did you hear about us?" or use tracking numbers).
5. **Double down on winners.**
   When a post, email, or offer obviously produces jobs, turn it into a repeatable campaign instead of a one-time event.

What to Measure in Marketing

To live out "you don't improve what you don't measure," track at least:

- **Leads per week**: calls, forms, DMs.
- **Booked jobs per week:** from those leads.
- **Average revenue per job.**
- **Source of leads:** social, Google, referrals, email, etc..

Even rough tracking beats guessing. Over time, you'll see which channels bring your best customers and where you're wasting effort.

Reflection Questions

- Is your business clearly visible and consistent wherever customers look for you online?
- Which 1–2 marketing channels are already working best, and how can you intentionally lean into them?
- What simple metrics will you start tracking this week to judge your marketing?
- If you had to design one 30-day campaign tomorrow, what would you promote, and how would you measure success?

What Matters Most

Marketing is not about shouting the loudest. It is about consistently putting clear, helpful messages in front of the right people—and then measuring what happens. Use simple, repeatable campaigns, show up daily on social, and track the numbers that matter. When you find something that works, go all in until it stops. That is how you turn random "word of mouth" into a marketing engine for your million-dollar service startup.

Chapter 3: When to Hire

Growing a service company from one truck to a real team is where many owners get stuck. You can grind your way to a certain level on your own, but you cannot build a million-dollar service startup by being the tech, the dispatcher, the salesperson, and the bookkeeper forever.

The Struggle of Doing It All

When Fabtech Solutions started, "team" meant me. I answered phones, ran service calls, handled quotes, ordered parts, did invoicing, and tried to squeeze in marketing at night. I kept a clean shirt in the truck so I could look like a salesperson after crawling out of a job.

It felt good to be needed, but I was the bottleneck. Calls were missed, estimates delayed, and important tasks pushed to "later," which never came. I told myself, "I'll hire when I can afford it," but the truth was the opposite: I couldn't afford not to hire if I wanted real growth.

Your ego has to take a hit here. You might be great at everything in your business, but if you keep clutching every task, you lock in your own ceiling.

Why Hiring Matters

Hiring is not just about getting more hands. It is about buying back your time so you can focus on the work only you can do: casting vision, building relationships, and steering the company. The right hire:

- Frees you from low-value tasks.
- Helps you take more (and better) jobs.
- Brings new ideas and energy.

The wrong hire, rushed in desperation, drains cash, morale, and your time. So, the goal is not "hire anyone;" it is "hire the right next person on purpose."

How to Know When the Time Is Right

You are probably ready to hire sooner than you think. Clear signs:

- You regularly turn down work because you are too busy.
- You miss calls or reply late to customers.
- You are making mistakes or cutting corners.
- Your family time and health are paying the price.
- The same fires keep flaring up because you are spread too thin.

If you see yourself in that list, it is time to create a hiring plan instead of waiting for some imaginary perfect moment.

Planning Your First (or Next) Hire

List every recurring task you handle in a week. Then mark:

- **$10-$20/hour work:** filing, scheduling, basic admin.
- **$20–$30/hour work:** standard field or shop work.

- **$100+/hour work:** sales, strategy, relationships, key decisions.

Your first hire should pull the lowest-value tasks off your plate so you can spend more of your time on $100+/hour work. For some owners, that's a tech; for others, it's an admin/CSR. Start where the pressure is highest.

Write a simple job description that covers:

- Main responsibilities
- Required behavior and attitude
- Basic schedule
- Starting pay and how raises/bonuses work

Run this by a mentor or peer you trust. Clarity now saves pain later.

Finding the Right Person

Skills matter, but in service businesses, **behavior and attitude** matter more. You can teach technical tasks; you cannot teach integrity or work ethic.

Screen for this in your interview questions:

- "Tell me about a time you solved a problem for a customer without being asked."
- "What does being on time mean to you?"
- "What kind of work environment do you do best in?"
- "If a customer is unhappy and you think they're wrong, what do you do?"

Red flags: blaming others, trashing previous employers, showing up late to the interview, or vague answers about goals.

Ask yourself two questions before hiring:

- Would I want to ride in a truck with this person all day?
- Would I trust them alone with my best customer?

If the answer is no, keep looking—even if you are busy.

Training New Team Members

Hiring does not end when someone signs paperwork. Untrained people are expensive. Set a 90-day onboarding plan:

- **Week 1–2:** shadowing, safety, basic processes, culture.
- **Week 3–4:** supervised work on defined tasks.
- **Week 5–12:** gradually increasing independence with clear performance targets.

Document how you want key tasks done (checklists, short videos, or simple SOPs). Encourage questions. Correct early and kindly. Check in weekly during those first 90 days.

Growing as a Leader

Every hire forces you to grow as a leader. Your job shifts from "doing all the work" to:

- Setting clear expectations.
- Giving feedback—positive and corrective.
- Removing obstacles so your people can win.

When problems show up, ask first: "Is this a person issue or a process issue?" Sometimes the employee is struggling because the system is unclear or broken. Fix the system before you assume the person is the problem.

Practical Steps for Hiring

- List out all tasks you do and circle the ones someone else could handle with training.
- Choose the single role that would free the most time or eliminate your biggest bottleneck.
- Write a one-page job description and share it with your network, team, and social media.
- Interview more than one candidate; never hire the first warm body because you are desperate.
- Use a 90-day probation period with clear goals and regular check-ins.

What to Measure Around Hiring

To avoid guessing, track:

- **Time to hire:** days from posting the job to accepted offer.
- **Retention:** how many new hires stay at least 6 and 12 months.
- **Ramp-up time:** how long it takes a new hire to reach full productivity.

- **Owner hours:** weekly hours you personally spend on field work vs. leadership/sales before and after hiring.

When these numbers improve, you will feel it in your schedule, your stress level, and your revenue.

Reflection Questions

- Where are you currently the bottleneck in your business?
- What tasks do you absolutely need to stop doing within the next 90 days?
- What role, if filled well, would unlock the most growth right now?
- How will you measure whether your next hire is successful?

Closing Thoughts

Hiring is one of the scariest steps in building a million-dollar service startup—but it is also one of the most important. You will feel the same fear you felt when you first launched your business. Do it anyway, but do it with a plan. Bring on the right person, train them well, measure the results, and you will unlock growth you simply cannot reach alone.

Chapter 4: When to Fire

Running a business means leading people—and sometimes the hardest part of leadership is knowing when someone can't stay. Firing is never fun, but holding on to the wrong person is far more expensive than letting them go. If you want a healthy, million-dollar service startup, you must learn to remove the wrong fit quickly and fairly.

Why Terminate Someone

Most people want to do a good job. But there are times when an employee:

- Consistently underperforms.
- Refuses to follow core processes.
- Damages team morale or your reputation.
- Will not take responsibility or improve.

Keeping someone in a role they can't or won't do well hurts your customers, your team, and the person themselves. They might be a better fit somewhere else, but as the owner, your first responsibility is to the health of the business and the people doing things right.

Signs It Is Time to Let Someone Go

Before firing, look for clear patterns, not one bad day. Warning signs:

- Repeated lateness, no-shows, or schedule games.
- Sloppy work that continues after coaching.
- Disrespect toward customers or coworkers.

- Negative attitude that drags down the team.
- Ignoring safety rules or company policies.
- No real change after honest feedback and written warnings.

If you've clearly communicated expectations, provided training, and documented issues—and things still don't change—it is time to act.

Firing Is Not About Anger

Firing should never be done in the heat of the moment. It is not about revenge or emotion; it is a business decision based on facts.

Before you terminate someone, make sure you have:

- A written job description and expectations.
- Documented conversations about performance or behavior.
- At least one formal warning outlining what must change and by when.

When you follow a process, firing is rarely a surprise to the employee. They may still be upset, but they should understand **why** it is happening.

The Right Way to Fire Someone

Here is a simple structure you can follow:

1. **Prepare.**
   Gather notes, warnings, and any HR documents.

Decide on final pay details and what company property needs to be returned.
2. **Choose the right setting.**
Meet in private, ideally with another leader or HR/office person present.
3. **Be clear and brief.**
Example script:
"We've talked several times about [specific issues], and we haven't seen the necessary improvement. Because of that, today will be your last day with the company."
4. **Explain next steps.**
Share when they'll receive their final paycheck, how to return keys/gear, and who they can contact with questions.
5. **Stay respectful.**
Avoid arguing or debating the decision. Stick to facts, not personal attacks. If appropriate, thank them for what they did contribute and wish them well.

Your goal is to be firm, fair, and professional—not cruel.

Learning From Every Firing

After letting someone go, review what led there. Ask yourself:

- Did we hire too fast or ignore red flags?
- Were expectations clear from day one?
- Did we provide the training and tools needed to succeed?
- Did we wait too long to address problems?

Sometimes a firing reveals a system problem—unclear procedures, inconsistent training, or a weak hiring process. Fix those so the next person has a better shot at winning.

Helping Your Team Move Forward

Firing someone affects the rest of the team. If you handle it well, your good employees will often feel relieved. If you handle it poorly, they may feel anxious or wonder if they are next.

You do not need to share private details, but you can say something like:

"[Name] is no longer with the company. We wish them well. Our expectations around [attendance/quality/attitude] remain the same for everyone. If you have questions about your role or expectations, talk with me directly."

Use this as a chance to reinforce standards and reassure your top performers that you will protect the culture.

Practical Tips

- Keep simple performance notes for each employee (attendance, issues, wins).
- Address problems early with a calm conversation instead of waiting until you're angry.
- Use a basic three-step process: verbal warning → written warning → termination.
- Apply policies consistently; don't make exceptions for "favorites."

- When possible, have one other person present during termination meetings or ensure the space is covered by security cameras for everyone's protection.

What to Measure Around Firing

To keep emotions out and improvement in, track:

- **Number of terminations per year** and main reasons (attendance, quality, behavior).
- **Time from first documented issue to termination.**
- **Percentage of terminations within the first 90 days of employment.**
- **Turnover rate:** how many employees leave (voluntary and involuntary) each year.

High early-stage terminations may mean your hiring or onboarding process needs work. Long delays between problems and action often signal leadership avoidance.

Reflection Questions

- Is there anyone on your team right now who consistently violates your standards or drains morale?
- Have you clearly documented expectations and given them a fair chance to improve?
- What fears keep you from letting the wrong person go sooner?
- How can you make your firing process more consistent, fair, and professional?

Closing Thoughts

Letting someone go is emotionally heavy, but avoiding it comes with a bigger cost. A single toxic or consistently underperforming employee can cap your growth, poison your culture, and push out your best people. Strong leaders do the hard things with clarity and compassion. When you combine clear expectations, real documentation, and firm follow-through, firing becomes what it should be—a necessary step to protect the business and the people who are doing things right.

Chapter 5: Attracting Talent

As your business grows, you do not just need more people—you need the **right** people. The difference between a stressful, always-on operation and a stable million-dollar service startup is usually the quality of the team. Behavior and attitude are the two traits that matter most. Skills and technical knowledge can be taught; character cannot.

Why Talent Matters

You can be the best technician in your market, but you will hit a ceiling if you are surrounded by mediocre or misaligned people. Great employees:

- Take ownership of problems.
- Treat customers like they're their own.
- Bring ideas that make your systems better.

The wrong employees create callbacks, destroy morale, and burn your time. Attracting the right talent is not a "nice to have"—it is one of your main jobs as a founder.

Common Mistakes When Attracting Talent

Many owners hurt themselves by:

- Hiring only friends or family because it feels safe.
- Focusing almost entirely on technical experience instead of behavior and attitude.
- Hiring desperately to "fill a seat" instead of waiting for fit.

- Ignoring how their company **looks** from the outside—online reviews, social media, and word of mouth.

The more intentional you are upfront, the less you'll spend on damage control later.

How to Attract the Right Talent

1. Show Off Your Company's Strengths

People want to work where they can grow, be respected, and feel part of something real. Get clear on what makes your shop different:

- Willingness to train from the ground up.
- Clear advancement paths and performance-based pay.
- A culture that values family, faith, and personal development.

Tell that story on your website, job posts, and social media. Your goal is to attract people who say, "That sounds like where I belong."

2. Use Word of Mouth and Social Media

Some of your best hires will come from:

- Current employees who invite friends.
- Customers who like how you operate.
- People who follow you online.

Let your team know exactly what role you are hiring and offer a referral bonus for successful hires. Post short videos describing the job, the kind of person who thrives at your company, and what growth can look like. Real faces and honest talk beat corporate-sounding job ads every time.

3. Make a Clear Job Posting

Don't just say, "Technician wanted. Competitive pay." That attracts everyone and no one. Instead:

- Describe the main responsibilities.
- Spell out the behaviors you expect (on-time, honest, coachable, customer-first).
- Mention training, advancement, and performance pay.

Example:
"Looking for a hardworking, teachable service tech who takes pride in their work and wants a long-term career, not just a job. We'll train the right person if the attitude is there."

4. Treat Each Candidate Well

Every candidate is either a future employee, a future customer, or someone who will talk about you. Respond quickly. Say thank you even when you pass. Be on time for interviews. The way you treat applicants is often the first culture signal they see.

5. Offer Training and Growth

Talented people care about where they're going. Show them:

- How they can move from helper → tech → senior tech → lead → manager.
- What training or certifications you'll pay for.
- How performance-based pay lets them out-earn their peers in other shops.

When people can see a path, they are far more likely to choose you and stay.

6. Reward Good Work

Money matters, but simple recognition matters too. Use:

- Public shout-outs in meetings or group texts.
- Small bonuses, gift cards, or a steak dinner for top performers.
- Special opportunities—better truck, better routes, or first shot at overtime.

These things cost little compared to turnover, and they reinforce the kind of behavior you want more of.

When You Can't Find Talent

If you feel like "no one wants to work," look at your approach:

- Are your wages and benefits competitive for your area and trade?
- Does your online presence (Google reviews, social media, Glassdoor) make you look like a place **you** would want to work?
- Are you only posting in one place, or are you using multiple channels: social, local schools, trade programs, churches, veterans' groups, job fairs?

Sometimes the problem is not the labor market; it's that good people do not know you exist yet.

What to Measure Around Attracting Talent

To avoid guessing, track:

- **Number of applicants per open role.**
- **Source of applicants:** employee referral, social media, job boards, schools.
- **Interview-to-hire ratio:** how many interviews it takes to find a "yes."
- **Retention of new hires at 6 and 12 months.**

If referrals produce high-retention hires, double down there. If a job board sends you a lot of low-quality candidates, either change the posting or drop it.

Reflection Questions

- Would you be excited to work for your company if you saw it from the outside?
- What is the **real** value proposition for employees who join your team?

- Which channel has given you your best hires so far—and how can you use it more intentionally?
- What one improvement could you make this month that would make your company more attractive to top talent?

Final Thoughts

Attracting talent is about more than filling open positions. It is about building a team of people who share your values, want to grow, and are willing to help you build something bigger than themselves. When you tell a clear story, treat people well, and measure what's working, your company becomes a magnet for the kind of talent that can carry you to (and beyond) your first million in service revenue.

Chapter 6: Employee Handbook

Every game has rules. So does every successful business. When expectations are clear and written down, people know how to win, leaders make better decisions, and drama goes down. An employee handbook is simply your playbook for how things work inside your company.

Why Rules and Policies Matter

Imagine playing football with no sideline, no end zone, and no idea what counts as a score. That's how many small businesses operate. Employees guess at:

- How they get paid and when.
- What the dress and safety standards are.
- How to ask for time off.
- What happens if they are late, no-show, or break a rule.

When you put these things in writing, you remove confusion. A good handbook protects the company, protects the team, and makes new hires feel safer and more confident on day one.

Common Mistakes with Handbooks

Owners often:

- Skip a handbook entirely and "wing it."
- Copy a giant corporate handbook that doesn't fit their small business.
- Never update policies as the company grows.
- Fail to actually **use** the handbook—employees never see it or can't access it.

You want something simple, clear, and alive—not a 60-page legal document no one reads.

How to Build Your Employee Handbook

Start with a few core sections written in plain language:

1. **Welcome, Mission, and Values**
   Why your company exists, what you stand for, and how you expect people to treat each other and customers.
2. **Roles and Expectations**
   Basic standards for behavior: showing up on time, communication, customer service, following procedures.
3. **Pay and Compensation**
   - How often people are paid.
   - How overtime, bonuses, and performance pay work.
   - How expenses and reimbursements are handled.
4. **Appearance and Safety**
   - Uniform or dress code.
   - PPE requirements.
   - Vehicle and tool standards.
5. **Attendance and Time Off**
   - Work hours and scheduling.
   - How to request vacation.
   - Sick time, no-call/no-show rules, and consequences.
6. **Discipline and Termination**
   - The steps: verbal warning → written warning → final warning → termination.
   - Examples of behavior that can lead to immediate termination (violence, theft, major safety violations).

7. **Use of Company Property**
    - Vehicles, fuel cards, phones, laptops, tools, and how they're to be used and cared for.

Keep each section short, concrete, and free of legal jargon. You can start from a free template, but customize every policy to match how you actually run the business.

Getting Feedback and Keeping It Alive

Once you draft a handbook:

- Review it with a local attorney or HR pro, if possible, especially around discipline and termination.
- Walk through it with your current team—ask what's unclear or unrealistic.
- Update it at least once a year as your systems and benefits evolve.

Make the handbook easy to access: printed copies in the office, a PDF link in a shared drive, and part of your onboarding for every new hire.

Communicating Expectations

A handbook no one understands or remembers is useless. When you bring someone on:

- Schedule time to go through key sections with them.

- Give real examples ("Here's what happens if you're late three times," "Here's how we approve overtime").
- Have them sign an acknowledgment page stating they received and understand the handbook.

During team meetings, reference the handbook when issues come up. This trains everyone to see it as the standard, not just a piece of paper.

Being Consistent and Fair

Once expectations are written, your job is to enforce them **consistently**:

- Same rules for everyone—no special treatment for top techs, family, or long-timers.
- When discipline is needed, use the steps outlined in the handbook instead of reacting emotionally.
- Document warnings and conversations so you can show what happened if a situation escalates.

Consistency builds trust. People can accept a "no" if they know the same rule applies to everyone.

What to Measure Around Policies

To see if your handbook is doing its job, track:

- Number of **attendance issues** per quarter.
- Number of **disciplinary write-ups** and most common reasons.

- **Turnover related to policy violations** (people fired for attendance, safety, or behavior).
- **Onboarding completion rate** (how many new hires complete handbook orientation and sign acknowledgments).

If the same problem keeps showing up in your notes—like repeated no-shows or confusion about time off—either your policy is unclear, your enforcement is weak, or the rule doesn't fit reality and needs to be adjusted.

Reflection Questions

- Does every employee in your company know where to find your current policies?
- Are there any "unwritten rules" that need to be written down and standardized?
- What is the number-one behavior or issue causing frustration today—and does your handbook address it clearly?
- What one change to your policies or communication would make life easier for both you and your team?

Final Thoughts

A solid employee handbook is not about control for its own sake. It is about clarity. It tells your team, "Here's how we win together and here's how we protect each other." When you write simple rules, communicate them clearly, and measure where breakdowns happen, you create a workplace that feels fair, consistent, and professional—and that's the kind of environment that keeps good people around as you build your million-dollar service startup.

Chapter 7: Pay — Performance-Driven Compensation

Pay is more than a paycheck. It's how you show people their work matters and give them a real reason to care about the numbers, not just the hours. When you tie compensation directly to results, your team stops thinking like employees and starts thinking like partners in the mission.

Performance-driven compensation is one of the most powerful tools you have for building a million-dollar service startup—if you keep it simple, fair, and crystal clear.

What Is Performance Pay?

Performance pay means part of someone's income is based on **what they produce**, not just the time they clock. That can look like:

- Commissions on sales or upsells.
- Bonuses for hitting revenue or profit targets.
- Revenue-sharing or profit-sharing based on measurable results.

At Fabtech Solutions, for example, our service technicians receive a share of the top-line revenue they are responsible for. That structure:

- Motivates them to maximize billable work and efficiency.

- Gives them control over their income.
- Removes the guesswork for "Christmas bonuses".

If you want a bigger bonus, you generate more revenue. Simple and fair.

Why Use Performance Pay?

Done right, performance pay:

- Aligns incentives. When the business wins, the employee wins.
- Drives better decisions. Techs think about quality, efficiency, and add-on opportunities.
- Helps retain top performers who know they can out-earn average people in other shops.

You'll know it's working when your team starts asking, "What can I do to move the numbers?" instead of, "Why didn't I get a raise?"

Common Mistakes to Avoid

Performance systems can backfire when owners:

- Make the plan too complicated to understand.
- Set targets so high that people give up.
- Change rules mid-year or move the goalposts.
- Don't track results accurately.
- Promise bonuses they later can't afford.

A simple plan you can explain on one page—and actually fund—is better than a fancy spreadsheet no one trusts.

Setting Up a Simple, Fair System

Start by answering three questions:

1. **What do you want more of?**
   Revenue, gross margin, 5-star reviews, low callbacks, on-time performance.
2. **Who can directly influence that?**
   Techs, sales reps, installers, CSRs, or whole crews.
3. **How will you pay for improvement?**
   A percentage of revenue, a flat bonus at certain milestones, or a team pool.

Then design the plan:

- **Choose 1–3 metrics per role.**
  Example for techs: monthly revenue produced, callbacks, and 5-star reviews.
- **Define the trigger and payout.**
  Example:
    - Base pay covers a healthy minimum.
    - Above $X in yearly revenue with zero callbacks, perfect attendance, and ten 5-star reviews = 1% gross revenue bonus.
- **Write it out in plain language.**
  One page, no fine print. Share it in your handbook and onboarding.

Walk through examples so everyone sees how the math works before you launch. If they can't explain it back to you, it's not clear enough.

Tracking Results and Giving Feedback

Performance pay only works if the math is real and visible. You must:

- Track the chosen metrics every week or month.
- Share results with employees so they see where they stand.
- Review numbers in one-on-ones and team meetings.

This is where "you don't improve what you don't measure" shows up again. When people see their numbers, they naturally ask how to improve them. Your job is to coach, not just judge.

If a tech is missing targets, dig into why:

- Do they need more training?
- Are they getting the right types of calls?
- Is your pricing or dispatching slowing them down?

Fix systems, not just people.

Supporting Employees Who Miss Goals

Performance pay should **motivate**, not punish. If someone is consistently below target:

- Meet with them one-on-one.
- Review their numbers and specific jobs.
- Identify one or two skills to improve (diagnostics, communication, upselling, time management).

- Set a short-term improvement plan with clear support—ride-alongs, training, scripts, or better tools.

If they show the right behavior and attitude, double down on coaching. If they refuse to improve or game the system, they may not be a fit.

Celebrating and Recognizing Success

When people crush it, make sure they feel it:

- Pay bonuses on time—never late.
- Publicly recognize top performers in meetings, texts, and group chats.
- Use non-cash rewards sometimes: steak dinners, gift cards, extra PTO, better trucks or routes.

Recognition builds a culture where winning is normal and visible.

What to Measure in Performance Pay

To keep your plan healthy, track:

- **Payout vs. profit:** total bonuses paid compared to margin.
- **Revenue per tech or per team.**
- **Callbacks and customer review scores.**
- **Turnover of high performers vs. average performers.**

If bonuses are high but profit is shrinking, adjust percentages or targets. If performance plans are barely paying out, you've made them too hard.

Reflection Questions

- What results matter most in your service company—and are you currently rewarding them?
- Can your employees clearly explain how they earn more money, or is it a mystery?
- Do you have the systems and reporting needed to track performance accurately?
- What is one simple performance-based element you can add to your pay structure in the next 90 days?

Final Thoughts

Performance-driven compensation is one of the strongest levers you have to connect your team's daily effort to your company's mission and metrics. Keep it simple, make it transparent, track it consistently, and adjust as you learn. When your people know exactly how to win—and get paid for winning—you're no longer dragging a team uphill. You're building a million-dollar service startup with a crew that's pulling with you.

Chapter 8: Systems and Numbers

Reaching your first million in service revenue is not about one giant client or one lucky year. It is about putting simple, repeatable systems in place and then watching the numbers so you can keep improving. Most service businesses stay stuck because they rely on memory, "common sense," or one superstar employee instead of documented processes.

If you want a business that runs with or without you, you have to get serious about systems and measurement.

Why Systems Matter

Systems turn chaos into something you can manage and grow. Without them:

- Every job is done "a little different" depending on who's on site.
- Customers get inconsistent experiences.
- Training new people feels like starting from scratch every time.

With basic, written systems, your company becomes easier to run, easier to scale, and easier to sell one day. You stop depending on heroes and start depending on processes.

Common Mistakes

Owners often:

- Keep everything in their head instead of on paper.

- Overcomplicate systems and never actually use them.
- Build processes once and never review or update them.
- Fail to connect systems to metrics, so no one knows if things are working.

The goal is not to create a corporate manual. The goal is to make it so that a reasonably smart person can follow your process and get a consistent result.

Start With Your Critical Paths

You don't need to document everything at once. Start with the few flows that matter most:

- **Lead to booked job:** how a stranger becomes a paying customer.
- **Job execution:** from arrival to completion and follow-up.
- **Cash collection:** invoicing, payment, and any follow-up on balances.

For each one, outline the steps in plain language:

1. Trigger (what starts the process).
2. Who is responsible at each step.
3. What tool or form they use (CRM, checklist, script).
4. What "done right" looks like (photos, signatures, payment collected, review requested).

Keep these on one page if possible. Use checklists and short bullets, not long paragraphs.

Make Systems Real for Your Team

A system only exists if your people know it and use it. To make that happen:

- Train new hires on the specific checklists they'll use, not just "how we do things."
- Review one process at a time in team meetings and ask, "What needs fixing?"
- Keep forms and templates easy to find—printed in the shop or saved on the Drive or a public folder/app.

When techs help improve a system, they're far more likely to follow it.

Numbers: What to Measure

This is where "you don't improve what you don't measure" comes back again. For a million-dollar service startup, track at least:

- **Leads per week** and where they come from.
- **Booked jobs per week** and close rate.
- **Average ticket** (revenue per job).
- **Callback rate** and warranty work.
- **Revenue and gross profit per tech or team.**

You don't need perfect software on day one. A simple spreadsheet or whiteboard works as long as you update it consistently.

Turning Data into Decisions

Numbers by themselves don't change anything—you have to respond to what they show:

- If leads are low but close rate is high, you have a marketing problem, not a sales problem.
- If callbacks are high, you have a quality or training problem.
- If revenue per tech is low, you may have a dispatch, pricing, or efficiency issue.

Pick one metric to improve each quarter. Build or adjust one system around that metric, train on it, and review the numbers regularly.

Practical Steps

- List your top three processes (lead to job, job execution, money collection). Write each as a simple checklist.
- Choose 3–5 key numbers you'll review every week and post them where the team can see.
- Schedule a monthly "systems meeting" to fix one bottleneck at a time instead of trying to fix everything at once.
- Tie at least one part of your performance pay or bonus plan to the numbers you're tracking.

Reflection Questions

- If you took a two-week vacation tomorrow, which parts of your business would fall apart first?
- Which core process (lead handling, job execution, or money collection) causes you the most stress right now?
- What are the three most important numbers that tell you whether your service company is healthy?
- What is one system you can document and one metric you can start tracking this week?

Final Thoughts

Systems and numbers are not the exciting part of entrepreneurship—but they are what separate a job from a real company. When you document the way you want things done and measure the results, you turn daily chaos into predictable progress. That's how you build a million-dollar service startup that can grow beyond you, not just because of you.

Chapter 9: Protecting Profit and Pricing your Service

Hitting $1,000,000 in revenue does not automatically mean you have a successful business. Too many owners cross that line on paper while still feeling broke, stressed, and behind on bills. Revenue is vanity. Profit and cash flow are what keep your service company alive.

This chapter is about protecting what you're building so the money actually shows up in your bank account—and stays there.

Why Profit Comes First

As you grow, it becomes easier to confuse "busy" with "profitable." More trucks, more jobs, more employees—yet the owner takes home less. That usually means:

- Pricing is too low.
- Costs are not being tracked.
- Cash is leaking through discounts, warranties, and sloppy systems.

Your million-dollar service startup needs profit on purpose, not as an accident at the end of the year. Profit is what funds growth, upgrades equipment, and gives you breathing room instead of constant anxiety.

Common Money Traps

Service owners often fall into the same traps:

- **Guessing on pricing.** Charging what "feels fair" instead of what covers labor, overhead, and desired profit.
- **Ignoring overhead creep.** Adding software, vehicles, and staff without checking ROI.
- **Letting accounts receivable pile up.** Doing jobs for weeks before collecting payment.

- **Not watching job-level performance.** Some services or customers may be unprofitable and you don't see it.

You cannot fix what you cannot see. That's why measurement matters so much here.

Know Your Numbers

At a minimum, you should track:

- **Monthly revenue** and **gross profit margin** (after direct labor and other COGs).
- **Overhead** (rent, softwares, admin, insurance, trucks, etc.).
- **Net profit**—what's truly left after everything.
- **Cash in the bank** and **weeks of operating expenses** you could cover if work stopped.

For a more detailed view, track revenue and profit **by service type or team** so you know what to scale and what to fix or kill.

You don't need to be a CPA. Use bookkeeping software like QuickBooks, a simple dashboard, or help from an accountant—but review these numbers at least monthly, if not weekly.

Price Like a Real Business

Your prices must cover:

1. Direct labor and cost of goods.

2. A fair cost for overhead.
3. A target profit margin.

If your tech takes two hours on a job and your labor cost is, say, $100/hour, you have $200 in labor before parts, trucks, and overhead even enter the picture. Build your prices around **realistic time and cost**, not best-case scenarios.

If that math makes your price higher than some competitors, good. Competing on being "the cheapest" is a fast way to stay small and broke.

Control Overhead and Creep

As revenue grows, go through your expenses at least quarterly:

- Cancel subscriptions you're not using.
- Ask vendors for better pricing once you've proven consistent volume.
- Watch for "nice to have" purchases that don't move the needle.

On the job side, protect profit by:

- Writing clear scopes of work.
- Training techs on what's included and what is an add-on.
- Charging appropriately for extra time, travel, parts, or complexity.

Giving away work kills margins and trains customers to expect more for less.

Tighten Cash Flow

Revenue does not matter if the money takes 60 days to show up:

- Collect payment at completion whenever possible.
- Take deposits for large jobs or if traveling outside your normal territory.
- Send invoices same-day and follow a consistent process for reminders and collections.
- Avoid letting any one customer owe you a large percentage of your total receivables.

Healthy cash flow lets you sleep at night and seize opportunities instead of begging the bank for help.

What to Measure Around Profit and Cash

To stay out of the dark, track:

- **Gross margin %** by month (and by service technician if you can).
- **Net profit %** by month and year.
- **Outstanding Accounts Receivables:** number of accounts overdue.
- **Cashflow:** cash in the bank less expenses

Set simple targets and adjust pricing, costs, or processes when you fall short.

Practical Steps

- Schedule a 60-minute finance review once a month—non-negotiable.
- Identify your 3 most profitable services and your 3 least profitable, and plan one change for each.
- Raise prices where margins are consistently thin and see how it affects both volume and profit.
- Build a small emergency fund in the business—aim first for one month of expenses, then two, then three.

Reflection Questions

- Do you know your true net profit from last month and last year?
- Which services, customers, or jobs feel busy but may actually be unprofitable?
- If work stopped today, how long could your business operate on current cash?
- What one change to pricing, costs, or collections would most improve your profit in the next 90 days?

Final Thoughts

Reaching a million in revenue is exciting—but keeping more of that money is what actually changes your life. When you price correctly, watch your margins, control overhead, and tighten cash flow, your business stops feeling fragile. It becomes stable, predictable, and worth all the effort you've put in. That's the real win of building a million-dollar service startup.

Chapter 10: Ticket Takers vs. Drivers

As your business grows, you start to see two types of people on your team. Both might show up on time and do their jobs, but they do not impact the business the same way. Understanding the difference—and leading them differently—is a big part of building a million-dollar service startup.

In this chapter, let's call them **ticket takers** and **drivers**.

Ticket Takers: Just Doing the Job

Ticket takers are the people who show up, run the work that's handed to them, and go home. They:

- Follow instructions but rarely think beyond the task.
- Do the minimum that's asked, not much more.
- Don't pay attention to sales opportunities, reviews, or long-term customer relationships.

Ticket takers are not necessarily bad employees. They can be steady and reliable. The danger is when your whole company is built around them. You end up with a business that only moves when you personally push it.

Drivers: Moving the Business Forward

Drivers, on the other hand, treat the business like it's partly theirs. They:

- Look for ways to solve extra problems for the customer and team.
- Protect your reputation and relationships.
- Spot add-on work that truly serves the client and grows revenue.
- Care about the numbers: callbacks, reviews, revenue, and efficiency.

Drivers are the people you want building crews, leading branches, and mentoring new hires. They don't just complete tickets—they create momentum.

How to Spot the Difference

Ask yourself:

- Who calls in with ideas or concerns before small problems become big ones?
- Who you'd send to your best customer without thinking twice?
- Who still brings you solutions instead of excuses when a day goes sideways?

Those are your drivers. Ticket takers tend to avoid responsibility, blame tools/customers/traffic for everything, and disappear when things get tough.

Turning Ticket Takers into Drivers

Not every ticket taker will become a driver, but some will—if you lead them well. Steps that help:

- **Show them the bigger picture.** Share basic numbers: revenue, reviews, callback rates. Explain how their work moves those metrics.
- **Give them a path.** Lay out how they can move from "tech" to "lead" to "manager," and what behavior/skills it takes.
- **Tie part of their pay to performance.** When they earn more for better results, mindset often shifts.
- **Coach, don't just correct.** Ride along, listen to how they talk to customers, and give specific feedback they can use on the next job.

If someone has the right attitude and work ethic, you can usually teach them how to think like a driver over time.

When a Ticket Taker Should Stay a Ticket Taker

Some people are happiest doing solid, predictable work without extra responsibility. That's okay—as long as:

- They meet your standards.
- They don't poison the culture.
- You don't rely on them for leadership roles they're not wired for.

Use them where they fit best: steady execution within a clear system, under a strong driver.

When It's Time to Move On

If someone refuses to grow, pushes back on any extra effort, and drags others down, you have to protect the team. You've already seen in earlier chapters how to handle coaching, warnings, and—if needed—termination. Leaving a resistant ticket taker in a key spot will cost you far more than replacing them.

What to Measure Around People

To keep emotion out and clarity in, track:

- **Revenue and gross margin by person or crew.**
- **Callbacks and customer complaints by person.**
- **5-star reviews that mention specific team members.**
- **Retention of high-performers vs. everyone else.**

Drivers usually show up clearly in these numbers. They bring in more revenue, have fewer callbacks, and get named in reviews. Ticket takers tend to flatline.

Practical Steps

- List your team and mark who is currently a ticket taker and who is a driver.
- Choose one potential driver to invest in over the next 90 days with extra coaching and opportunity.
- Adjust your pay and recognition systems so drivers feel it when they win.
- Be honest about any long-term ticket takers who are hurting momentum and decide what needs to change.

Reflection Questions

- Who are the top drivers on your team right now, and how can you keep them for the long haul?
- Who are the long-term ticket takers holding back your culture or customer experience?
- What specific behaviors separate drivers from everyone else in your company?
- What is one change you can make this month to reward driver behavior and reduce tolerance for harmful ticket-taker behavior?

Final Thoughts

You can't build a strong service company on your own. You need people who will carry the mission with you. When you understand the difference between ticket takers and drivers—and you measure, reward, and coach accordingly—you stop pushing the business uphill by yourself. You start building a team that pulls with you toward that first million in service revenue and beyond.

Chapter 11: Bringing It All Together

Reaching your first $1,000,000 in service revenue does not come from one genius idea or one lucky break. It comes from stacking small, consistent actions in the same direction over time. This book has walked through leadership, marketing, hiring, firing, attracting talent, policies, pay, pricing, and sales—all through the lens of real experience, not theory.

If you haven't started your service business yet, treat this chapter as your launch blueprint. These are the systems and numbers you want to sketch out before you order your first shirts or wrap your first truck. Decide now how you'll attract leads, how you'll price, what "a good job" looks like, and what you'll track each week once the phone starts ringing. Building with this end in mind helps you skip a lot of the chaos most owners fight through in their first few years and move toward your first $1,000,000 in revenue with far more intention.

The goal here is simple: leave you with clarity on **what to do next** and **how to measure whether it is working**.

Your Million-Dollar Service Engine

Think of your business as an engine made of connected parts:

- **Leader:** your mindset, discipline, and willingness to grow.
- **Marketing and sales:** how you create and convert opportunities.

- **Operations:** how consistently and profitably you deliver work.
- **People:** who you hire, keep, develop, and sometimes let go.
- **Systems and policies:** the rules and checklists that keep everyone aligned.
- **Numbers:** the scoreboard that tells the truth about performance.

If one part is weak, the whole engine struggles. Your job is not to perfect every area at once. Your job is to find the weakest link, improve it, then move to the next—over and over again.

Build a 12-Month Roadmap

Instead of trying to fix everything in a weekend, break the next year into **four 90-day sprints**. For each quarter, choose:

1. **One primary focus area.**
   Marketing, recruiting, training, systems, pricing, or profit.
2. **One or two key metrics.**
   Weekly leads, callbacks, revenue per tech, or net profit percentage.
3. **Three to five concrete actions.**
   For example: launch one new campaign, document the service checklist, hire and onboard one tech using the new process.

Sample roadmap:

- **Quarter 1 – Marketing**
  Focus: qualified leads.
  Metrics: leads per week, close rate.
  Actions: build a basic campaign calendar, post consistently on social media, track how every lead finds you.
- **Quarter 2 – Operations**
  Focus: reduce callbacks and warranties.
  Metric: callback rate.
  Actions: standardize job checklists, create a simple dispatch process, train techs on expectations, customer sign off sheets.
- **Quarter 3 – People**
  Focus: hire and keep stronger players.
  Metrics: number of quality applicants, 90-day retention.
  Actions: refine job postings, create a structured interview, tighten onboarding.
- **Quarter 4 – Profit**
  Focus: protect margins and cash.
  Metrics: gross margin, net profit, days to collect payment.
  Actions: adjust pricing, review overhead, tighten billing and collections.

This keeps you moving without spreading yourself so thin that nothing actually changes.

Establish a Weekly Rhythm

Plans only matter if they show up in your week. A simple rhythm:

- **Weekly scorecard review (30–60 minutes).**
  Look at your key numbers: leads, jobs, average ticket, callbacks, revenue, profit, and any people metrics you're focused on.
- **One improvement project at a time.**
  Each week, move one system forward—update a script, refine a checklist, train one process, or clean up a report.
- **Invest in your people.**
  Have at least one intentional one-on-one, ride-along, or coaching conversation every week, using the tools from your hiring, firing, and pay chapters.

Protect this rhythm like you would a high-value customer. It is where real transformation happens.

Your Core Scoreboard

To live out the principle "you don't improve what you don't measure," keep a simple, visible scoreboard. At minimum, track:

- Leads per week.
- Jobs completed per week.
- Average revenue per job.
- Callback or warranty rate.
- Revenue and gross profit per tech or team.
- Net profit percentage each month.

Use a whiteboard, spreadsheet, CRM, or software—whatever you'll actually update. Review trends, not just individual days. When a number drifts in the wrong direction, ask:

- Is this a **marketing** issue (not enough opportunity)?
- An **operations** issue (poor execution or systems)?
- A **people** issue (wrong fit or untrained person)?
- A **pricing/profit** issue (we're too cheap or too slow)?

Your scoreboard points you to the real problem so you fix the cause, not just the symptoms.

Expect Resistance and Keep Going

As you implement what you've learned, expect resistance—from employees, from circumstances, and from your own habits. Some people will not like clearer standards. Some will push back on performance pay. Some will test whether you're serious about policies you used to ignore.

That tension is normal. It's also a sign that you're actually changing something. Your job is to:

- Stay firm on the **destination**: a healthy, profitable, million-dollar service company.
- Stay flexible on the **methods**: adjust systems and tactics as you learn.
- Own your mistakes, make changes, and keep moving.

You did not start this journey to be average. You started because something in you believed there was more.

Reflection and Next Steps

Before you close this book, answer these questions:

- Which chapter exposed your biggest current gap?
- What are the **three numbers** you will start tracking this week?
- What is the single most important change you will make in the next 30 days?
- Who can you share your plan with so you're not walking this road alone?

Write your answers down. Then put the first step on your calendar.

Final Words

You now have a practical playbook born from real wins, real mistakes, and real lessons in the field—not from a classroom or a boardroom. You have everything you need to start, grow, and lead a million-dollar service startup that takes care of your customers, your team, and your family.

The rest is up to you: measure, adjust, and keep showing up.

www.ingramcontent.com/pod-product-compliance
Lightning Source LLC
Chambersburg PA
CBHW050705160426
43194CB00010B/2014